SLOW WAR

T0158431

THE HUGH MACLENNAN POETRY SERIES

Editors: Allan Hepburn and Carolyn Smart

slow war

Benjamin Hertwig

McGill-Queen's University Press
Montreal & Kingston • London • Chicago

ISBN 978-0-7735-5142-8 (paper)
ISBN 978-0-7735-5175-6 (ePDF)
ISBN 978-0-7735-5176-3 (ePUB)

Legal deposit third quarter 2017
Bibliothèque nationale du Québec

Printed in Canada on acid-free paper that is 100% ancient forest
free (100% post-consumer recycled), processed chlorine free

McGill-Queen's University Press acknowledges the support of the
Canada Council for the Arts for our publishing program. We also
acknowledge the financial support of the Government of Canada
through the Canada Book Fund for our publishing activities.

Library and Archives Canada Cataloguing in Publication

Hertwig, Benjamin, 1985–, author
  Slow war / Benjamin Hertwig.

  (Hugh MacLennan poetry series)
  Poems.
  Issued in print and electronic formats.
  ISBN 978-0-7735-5142-8 (cloth). – ISBN 978-0-7735-5175-6 (ePDF). –
  ISBN 978-0-7735-5176-3 (ePUB)

  I. Title. II. Series: Hugh MacLennan poetry series

  PS8615.E777S66 2017   C811'.6   C2017-903538-X
                                      C2017-903539-8

This book was typeset by Marquis Interscript
in 9.5/13 New Baskerville.

CONTENTS

the same games that we played in dirt, in dusty school yards
have found a higher pitch and broader scale
– John K. Samson

GENESIS

behind the elementary school
and the great wooden structure
that looks like Noah's ark
I watch you kick
the dark-haired boy
in the stomach.
you kick him more than once.
you are familiar with violence.
he started it, you say
　I nod.
his spit and blood are on my cheeks,
wet sand and afternoon rain.

the car is running.   headlights flare past

swamp spruce
          phosphorescence   and *blaue stunde* shadows.

your opa unsnaps   a blade   from the sheath stitched
          permanently to his side.

          the car's comfortable warmth folds

into metallic cold,
          diesel fumes float   above gravel contours.

     I want you to see, he says.

the bump had been small, nothing
     to signify this new   horror, limbs twitching in silent orgasm,
     head snapping   back and forth across dry
  winter grass.

he places his foot
          on the neck and pulls   across.

  the motion stops.

          he washes   red hands in the snow,
               wipes the blade on felt pants.

the sky is mute and you are twelve.

it had to be this way, he says.

BUSH TRAILS

one foot follows the next past
    midwinter snow on spruce and pine –

you hold your rifle close
    as the lover you haven't

had yet and break
    through the ice

without words. *the water holds*
    the shape of your body,

the memory of slowly falling
    snow.

strong hands strip you.
    boots and clothes on snow.

you fall asleep to the hiss
    of the kerosene stove,

shadows dancing on canvas,
    the smell of sweat and cold.

you wake to a wall of flame,
    a burning tent.

bodies crashing in the dark.
        constellations pricking your

eyes. bare feet and midwinter
        snow on spruce and pine.

skunkmusk and alfalfa
drive-thru teenburgers
the long straight line
through fields and
barbed wire fenceposts
grain elevators
swimming in clover
asphalt and glass under
the city's halogen halo.
homesmell up till midnight
finishing *Harry Potter*
and the Prisoner of Azkaban
sitting on your bed
wondering if you
   will be afraid
when you see blood
and if you die
   will you be saved
and the girls at school
   will like you more
for having gone to war.

DRUNK-DRIVING

i.

there was a time you
drove home
                drunk
but didn't consider it as such
for you were going overseas
in a matter of weeks.

ii.

come to the drop-in centre,
the man at church said.

it'd be good for the boys
to see a man in uniform.

iii.

the street kids ran
from the uniform
until you changed

into something
    else,

and walked to the
rink
together,

jeans crinkling
in the cold.

iv.

the three of you
chose to wear
women's skates
because you
          could.

the picks at the front
          made
the three of you
fall
          all over
the ice.

the halogen
lights made
sure   everyone
saw.

Chris and Junior
thought
it was funny
          as hell.

v.

the bruises
on your knees
didn't matter
because you
were leaving
          for Afghanistan
in a matter of
days

and the boys
   were used
   to bruises.

vi.

you woke early.
the snow was
    deep.

your mother made strong
tea for the drive to war.

the boys
didn't want you to
        go.

the night before

they held onto
your arms –

you felt like
a father.

you liked them
and skating
too.

not the idea
of being a father
quite
       yet.

you got on the plane.

in your memory
it was still dark.

in your memory
you didn't
fall asleep

        at all.

vii.

in your memory
the boys
weren't
used to
being left

      behind.

EMERGENT

somewhere high over the Hindu
Kush the soldier across from you
reaches into a pocket,
pulls out a strip of bacon
borrowed from that morning's
breakfast. he places it into
his mouth with a smile,
receives laughter in exchange.
and after: the return to silence,
the primordial hum of the plane's
belly like Leviathan pulsing in
dark underwater cosmologies
or Marduk showering the earth
with his seed. now the soldiers
thinking of blow jobs or the return
to safe domestic spaces. now the ramp
opens with a whine like a pack of
bush dogs now the light hits your eyes –
you see land.

you pitch past market
  stalls backlit
like nativity grottos
  in prairie
catholic churches

where men in bare
  feet knead flour
into naan
  share tea
the news of the day

swerve around
  skitter of dogs
garbage and meatsmoke
  wide-eyed children
pastel fade of night

traffic circle
  circumference
throws the edges
  of equilibrium
then lets go

open road
  acceleration
deceleration
  washing machine hum
roadside fires

milk-cool air
  days after christmas
blanket weight
  of protective plates
on your chest

like the smell of rain
  and woodsmoke
in your parents' backyard
  like a mother
puts you to sleep.

RUMOURS, FORWARD OPERATING
BASE WILSON

in Helmand province the british soldiers tell you of the
taliban, how they tied two young troopers to the bumper of
a truck, dragged them through the desert till the blood fled
their bodies and the sand dried red; how a sniper from
Chechnya stalks the hills in devil's flesh and devours men
at a distance. you like these stories best – they are Grimm's
märchen. you taste iron on your tongue when they say *blood*
and you feel the sniper's gaze on the back of your neck as
you drive. but they are just stories. and stories are for the
slow hours at night when memory coagulates and you need
to stay awake, or for noon when the sun is brightest and
you need to fall asleep. stories are for pain. you wish
to understand.

GUARD TOWER, KANDAHAR

i.

the dutch soldier shows
you a photo of his
girlfriend's breasts
which are firm like
a melon, he laughs:
is that the right word?
twenty feet underfoot
jingle trucks shuffle in queue
like christmas lights
unfurling at the
bottom of a cardboard box.

ii.

soldiers rifle through
trucks, poking heads in
and placing mirrors
  under
food and batteries
discarded
drivers waved
into dust.

iii.

months later,
a burning truck
on highway one:

> imagine the driver,
> whether his naan
> and double AA's
> were tossed
> while you watched
> from above and wonder:
> is his body burning
> too.

ASH WEDNESDAY, FREEDOM
CHAPEL KANDAHAR

slide your rifle
     under the pew,

hold your hat
     in your hand.

female and male
     he created,

death and ubiquitous
     dust, *from dust you've*

come, to dust
     you shall be born

again, in oil and
     ashes, the sign of

the cross, red sun
     smoke and blood

your forehead
     marked with fire.

SALAT

the muezzin
calls the city
to prayer.

his agile voice
           lingers
like a flock
           of sparrows

in flight.

the convoy crosses
into Kandahar.

FIRST SHOT

you could have   been
playing   basketball on the asphalt,

the surface of   the road
pocked like   the skin of your

best friend
in eighth grade. last vehicle in the convoy,

backwards facing

machine gun   trolling for
signs.   jingle trucks and corollas,

a yellow taxi   follows   so

close   you can see   eyewhite

as he talks
on the phone.

hands waving,   bites into an apple,

not looking like
a killer,
your order is to shoot.

you shout   throw a bottle of

water,   the driver does not notice.

you wave your arms stop or

       I will shoot stop or I will shoot stop
you fucking idiot   stop stop stop.

       bullets snap into   cement

and the taxi slams to a
                          halt.
he looks in your eyes,   you cannot classify his expression,

you've never   felt this way before shame   euphoria,   the first

time you saw a body without clothes,   your order was to shoot.

face bleeding,
flap of skin
      size of a communion wafer

flecks of strawberry
blood like a wren's
      egg.

words weave around
      wind rows
of cigarette
      smoke.

reams of hot afternoon sky
 a posture of fear

clutching god to your chest
      like you love him you fear him you love him.

mountains in the distance

      sand between

grab your black
leather bible

hide
in the shade of truck

      tires.

head against sand
eyes on the book of
genesis
        fall asleep.

dream of a ladder
high in the sky
      and prayer flags

          snapping in the wind.

wake to sand between
silk white pages,
      nothing much to say.

she drove an old mercedes
  ate ice cream

played beach volleyball.
  in a week you were going back

to war and you wanted her more
  than you wanted the dead

to come back to breath
  or the sun to warm again.

you were twenty
  and her accent was german:

she would never write letters
  you would never write back.

ROOFTOP, PANJWAI

o lente, lente currite noctis equi
                    – Ovid

fireflare in the distance. full moon traces a slow parabola
        across the roof like running a finger through tabletop salt.
try to stay awake. the river flows, children gone home for
        the night. barking dogs and moist foliage, the smell of stale
piss. an afghan soldier in sandals and a *partug* reaches out a
        four-fingered hand, offers you a pipe. you shake your head,
no. hashsmoke floats across the roof. he smiles, sits back on
        the metal-framed bed, pats the horse-hair mattress, shrugs
his shoulders, falls asleep.

the sergeant drives you to
the front of the firefight like
a dad dropping you off
on the first day of school.

a chance for you to pop your combat cherry

he says as you flip
off safe, fire a few
rounds at the mud wall
and hope for a hooded
taliban target to appear.
a head flashes past window
frames: you fire a few more.
the sergeant slaps you
on the back and smiles.

that a boy, he grins, *get right into it good.*

EVENING AT A BURNT-OUT SCHOOL
WITH THE TENTH MOUNTAIN DIVISION

sitting in half-circle formation the first sergeant shares why
he dropped out of school: *kicked a teacher in the ass*, why
he has a hatchet, *half-american indian*, he laughs. faceless,
taliban farmers burned then abandoned the building you
will sleep in tonight. dope grows tall in the shade by the
trickling stream until plucked by the soldiers with gardener's
thumbs. they tuck sprigs into chest rigs like old men
rummaging gardens for summer salad fixings. so you walk
around the yard and share words with a duck that honks in
some strange tongue, sticking bill into ash and stirring
the dirt. so you poke the hedgehog that curls into a dusty
globe at your feet, spine curled like a child's, so snipers
perch on the roof like sinewy crows so you fall asleep to
laughter the smell of something someone burning.

SKOAL

the corporal lifts his
lower lip, tucks in a
wad of apple skoal
like he's planting
a garden.
a line of spittle
thin as a spider's web
dangles from his chin,
tobacco fibres rest
on the edges of his
army regulation
moustache.
he sips
coke and spits
certainty
gravel theodicies –
he loves his god
as he loves his family
this war.

EASTER SUNDAY, FORWARD OPERATING
BASE WILSON

sunrise dust and radio static cutting
    across
memories of your grandparent's farm:
    paska,
milk-bread, and last year's peppermint tea.
    dogs winding
through legs to the record scratch of *sacred head*
    now wounded,
the smell of vinegar on eggs of many colours.
    willow and elder
foreground, the horizon's shallow haze blending
    with
the slow smoulder of diesel fuel, burning
    shit.
the satellite phone is yours for an hour –
    your parents
aren't home, sisters sleeping in strange
    time zones.
answering machines and digital silence.
    a number rises
up from god knows where. three years and a war
    since last
you spoke. his parents pick up the phone:
    he's moved away,
they say. *happy easter, the lord is risen, take care, stay safe,*
    we'll say you called.

FRUIT ON A WOODEN TABLE

in the broken
  calm of four walls
and floor of earth

you have seen
  visions and bodies
in flame

the body of christ
  shed for you do not
belong. gunfire and

bombsong you do not
  belong. her eyes are
coal a face of wind

the place you stand
  is holy ground.
take off your boots

point your rifle
  towards the floor
and leave the way

you came
  through the kicked-in
wooden door

past the table
 with a bowl
of fruit.

you stand at attention.
he walks between the
soldiers, row by row,
stopping to ask the odd
woman or man where they
are from, how long
they have been away,
whether they have visited
the new tim horton's
yet. you are surprised
by the way his belly
protrudes, like a swollen
dog's stomach. pale winter
of his face swaying like
fishflesh on the bottom
of the ocean floor.
he wears a vest of many
pockets and as he passes
by you cannot imagine
whose lives   what life
the pockets contain.

CARE PACKAGE, KANDAHAR

the package is waiting on your bed
nested in mottled green of sleeping
bag and ranger blanket –
box the colour of sand,
packing tape, familiar ligature
of your father's sharpie scrawl.
flick the knife you bought at the PX,
operation enduring freedom
flashes across the blade
then sinks into cardboard flesh.

> a set of coloured pens
> a handwritten card
> with a psalm
> gummy coke bottles
> chocolate cookies
> a photograph 8 × 10 smooth,
> your childhood church.
> smell of hot wax and communion wine
> congregation splayed under altar
> next to the cross a reproduction
> of William Holman Hunt's *Light of the World.*
> the children hold a homemade banner
> *god bless you Benjamin,* they say.

see the sun in their hair,
touch the stone of their blessing.
place the photo face down
then bury it back in the box.

HOMEWARD

you pissed yourself
on the way home

Dubai's tall towers
city of light

naked skin on
wet white sheets

warm as the water
you had to drink

in the desert
warm as foaming

ocean white sand
beaches the lonely

lounging soldiers
hold novels

bright umbrellas
cold drinks

children splash
gulls cry at last

light.

the war is over
and we are still

    here.

if the good
angel had told
Faustus to go fuck
himself,
the metaphysical
baggage of war
and peace,
heaven and hell
would have
spilled out on the
dark floor of
the study like
a bowl of
peanut shells.
but the angel spoke
of love and the
pitchforked devils
dragged him
down. the war
is over and we
are still

    here.

FOOD HABITS OF COYOTES, AS DETERMINED
BY EXAMINATION OF STOMACH CONTENTS

i.

in northern Louisiana the coyote eats persimmon
flesh sweet, skin taut
and winter coyotes across America

eat more rabbit than any time
of the lunar year.
in central Alberta the coyote eats snowshoe hare

the kind that lives behind the anglican church
near your house
and turns white after first frost.

ii.

the muezzin calls the city
to prayer

       again.

like a flock of sparrows
in flight

       the convoy

crosses the river into
Kandahar.

       you wait.

iii.

a pack of six coyotes
wanders across the street

     streetlights and falling snow

you want to know what things they've
eaten in half-lit alley tracks

     what breath consumed.

iv.

murmuration of
muscle
like sparrows
over the North
Saskatchewan

swallows across the
Arghandab
ventricular red sex
and words like
glomerulus

a cluster of nerve
endings, blood
vessels.

words that signify
what has been
contained, what

      spilled

v.

you alone were on the street
when the last dipped head
tucked tail and
folded into winter brush.

still it snowed.

vi.

simile and metaphor –

tracks to get around
the fact
that the suicide bomber
was effective,
that coyotes eat what they can,
that a man's head was split
bright like persimmon and
a foot was resting on the road
like a bird with a broken
                wing.

TINNITUS, OR THE DRIVE-THRU WINDOW WHEN YOU RETURN

i.

some noises never leave
                your mind.

a week after your return
you uncover
a combination of items

on the breakfast menu

that when added together
(along with applicable taxes)

comes to
    $6.66

an eschatological, arbitrary
amount of food.

ii.

the man who takes your money has scars
all the way up his arms,

skin exposed like christ's watery
side on the cross

scars bright as a cut
goat's throat

the accumulation of white scratches
on the belly of a whale.

he passes down a sack of food,
wishes you a good day.

he means it.

you desire the same
for him

for yourself

though the ringing in your
ears has increased.

iii.

you eat, you drive.

this is the fallow of your mind:

a fallen eargplug at a weapons range
when the ringing first
began

a young man walking the cusp
of a beaver dam

   water
      spilling

over the flowing edge
   of a horizontal earth

winesick Hesiod staring at
the shield of Heracles,
predicting war

and the second
explosion –

the one you've written
so many stories about.

iv.

all this has brought
you here:

to the drive thru window –

the meat in your mouth
curdling into
   a slow scream

the muezzin calls
the city to prayer
again

dark birds
   flapping

surface
      tension

sun set
      moon
rise

the ringing

   you swallow.

VEHICLE IN FLAME

your catalogue of war photos
contains the image
of a vehicle in flame –

plumes of smoke
        black as the fires of Kuwait

that flared on the big screen

when you were seven.
the sky is purple,

colour of ash.

two soldiers in sand
uniforms carry
a wounded third outside

                        the frame.

you do not know how
you acquired this photo.
you do not know these men.
you were not by those rocks

        at that time.

YOUNG SOLDIER

peach-flavoured chewing
tobacco,
sun-sweet skin
and boot polish grease

      on knuckle creases

      like
you've been peeling the
flesh off chickens again.

bare asphalt under
your sixteen year
old self

watch bodies pile up in
the back of afghan national
army trucks,

tailgate blood drips

      into the riparian zone
         of the map,

exactly what you expect
cause war fucks with geography,

reconfigures
 the contour

 lines

 of your
 mind.

childhood fevers and the downspout
in the centre of the basement that
textures hallucination,
the rushing voice of god.

evening rain that

>   tap
>   tap
>   taps

the soft touch of your mother
and the wood-panelled wall
where you turn your face
for comfort when you sleep.

now you no longer hear voices
in fevers –
just limbs and faces and places
you've slept.

stone cairns

piled
    on
                old
love.

your heart would
climb the downspout
again

  see angels

                  ascending
            descending

say, *god is here!*

(that house is gone,
the downspout
torn out like a throat)

marry   the first person
who asks you not to
go.

fold   in the dead
with flour and
yeast.

watch   the dough
rise, wash your
hands.

wonder   where the
rifle's weight has
gone.

APPLE-PICKING, AFTER AFGHANISTAN

for all
that struck the earth
no matter if not bruised or spiked with stubble
went surely to the apple-cider heap

– Robert Frost

you met her after the war, got
married, went apple-picking.
she never understood why
as a grown man
you pissed yourself when
you left Afghanistan, so you
never told her about the time
you pissed yourself when
you left Afghanistan.
you were supposed to
pick fruit: you fought
a lot instead.
the mosquitoes lived much
longer than usual, well
after first frost.
the apple-drunk wasps nipped
at your
ankles like dogs.
all these things happened
in the fall –
the time things are
supposed to die.
one night you walked

the orchard together,
had sex
to the smell of rotting apples,
windy, dry leaves.
you slept in a volvo
outside the catholic
church and ran the car
to keep the cold
away.
you felt her body in
the dark.
the spire scratching
the firmament.
the car is covered
with frost
when you awake.
you are still
asleep,
waiting for war
to end.

WINTER BUCK

she is gone –

you are a hind-shot buck,
adrenaline sour

      meat spoiled
 crashing   through trees,

red drops in the snow.
each lesion   expands

try to convince yourself that the smell
      of bodies in your bed

comes from meat cooking
      in the room above   or foliage
decomposing outside your
bedroom   window.

like smoke   you slip
      into casual dream

violence where you push
old friends   out of moving

vehicles, sleep   with
      strangers

      fall into
and out of   sleep.

and now you are tired.
you are   not the pain

in your hands
or the sun on your face.
        so you follow

crop circles of hair
that lead   from legs

to thighs   and   chest:
a body   a room.
flickering   sentience   light   and sound.

ALTERNATE

it would have been easier
to die in Afghanistan
          under cover of flames

                    smoke the colour of sand,

tendons snapping
          burning

                    sexless ecstasy

of release –
now you envy

                    the dead.

DESIRE IN SEVENS

i.

pace across city streets under the full light of moon
like the coyote in winter, coat the colour of dirty snow
not knowing one day beyond
the next, moving with unconscious,
habitual desire, carrying only
the fear of loud noises
and an intimate knowledge of the cold.

ii.

return to a time
when you thought about
something
other than pain
or the tapping of trees
on your window.

iii.

strain
for intinction
in the cry
of every magpie
and crow.

iv.

make love
to anyone
with a kind
face

v.

watch yourself
sleep
from a distance

vi.

lay your head on soft
skin

vii.

wait without speech –

A COMPENDIUM OF HANDS

i.

in Dürer's most
reproduced woodcut
the hands join
     lightly

two herons curving
toward the same

     horizon line

dorsal veins run down
     the wrist

at ninety degrees

warm rivers cross the body's
continental divide.

ii.

in sleep

a hand is like   a foot
when it has been

      blown off

awkward angles
and digits grasping
towards a meaning
its form no longer
comprehends.

a man was in the ditch
when you brought him
a bottle of water.

hand warm
as sun-blanched
asphalt.

the muezzin's song

      floats

like dust motes
blown crosswise
by a pigeon's
wing.

iii.

you are these:

chunks of meat separated
by packing and
        refrigeration.

bones rattling against
                bones
and root of tree.

iv.

you met Omar Khadr
at a camping store
while trying to find
a tent –

his one eye translucent
like spilled

      countertop milk.

recall the restaurant man,
burger in hand:

Omar Khadr should rot in jail
for the rest of his days

you reach out and shake
Omar's hand.

this is not the hand of a man
who should rot in jail.

you leave without the
      tent.

v.

or the night you slept
on the ledge of a castle
wall in Croatia,

      legs dangling   overlooking the ocean.

after dark two men
 stepped
over your body:

        you awoke.

they were young and drunk
with shiny pointed shoes.

one touched your shoulder
with the back of his

hand –

      perhaps the hand of
god.

they kept walking and you:

you were dreaming of a
hand on the road.

you hadn't been touched
in months.

the afghan soldier transfixed by his feet,
staring, as if his eyes could put the blood
back in. his *partug* torn, blood-slick and beet
red. he calls out to someone; walls of mud
surround him. arterial blood, a flood
of red life. you touch his head; he's pretty
much dead already. eyes closing, the bud
of poppy blooms, cut. leave this city.
your short war is over; do not pity
the dead. buy yourself a new car – or tell
the truth. tales of how stupid and shitty
war is. how you pissed yourself, how he fell.
how in your dreams his face floats in motion:
fish flesh on the bottom of the ocean.

PORTRAIT OF A FAMILY FRIEND
IN YOUR BEDROOM, SIGNED CAMP HALLEIN
$(21/10/45)$

i.

he died years before your war.
you thought Hallein was
in Florida, close to the ocean,
the cry of gulls.

a google search:

thousand-year-old salt mine
funding the archbishopric
of Salzburg.

an overflow camp for Dachau.

ii.

his face in profile like
a sculpture in relief –

cheekbones high, eyes wide,
            neck straight.

as though to remind
himself that he is not

in the grave
            yet.

he sits for thirty years
in the wooden back pew

refusing to sing
            the hymns

but standing

                    sitting

            standing

along
with everyone else.

iii.

after the war
he leaves

children
       lovers
  sachertorte

tears   himself
       across inkblot ocean

to fields consumed
       by sky and snow,

breath slow.
       summer wind stirring
           an overflowing ashtray

a forty every
week

       near

the farm in Mayerthorpe
where four

mounties eventually
die
in the dark.

he too is dead now
but first

for thirty years
grew a garden:

beans, tomatoes
kohlrabi and cabbage.

iv.

his portrait is next to
your bed.

his eyes stare straight
                past the frame
        and into your room.

scanning the walls
where his eyes could meet

those of the horse in the Alex Colville
print

the train is approaching

        approaching

the sky is grey.
nothing much is growing
at all.

you cannot see the horse's eyes,

only the smoke of the train,
the curve of the track.

the sightless white lens of approaching

        motion

the horse runs straight
        ahead.

74

"blaze engulfs boston pizza, blockbuster" –
the Prince George story the morning after
you noticed the smoke and burning plastic.
this same morning the pine beetles ravish
the forests you are trying to replant
and the special forces prepare to kill
Osama Bin Laden, though he doesn't
know it yet. you don't know it yet either.
an old woman pokes her head into your
motel room, shouts: *they got Bin Laden, shot
him through the fucking head.* the streetlights on
fifteenth and Victoria change from red
to yellow to green grass under your feet.
Afghanistan feels very far away.

THE LITURGICAL LEAP INTO MONDAY, OR SOME OF THE THINGS YOU WISH YOU'D TOLD YOUR GRANDFATHER

i.

one sunday after your
or my war
you leapt across the grave –
clear across
black robes flapping like a bird.

this isn't a metaphor for resurrection:
the grave was real with a body inside.
you were presiding the liturgy.
the grave was collapsing.
you didn't wish to fall in.

you leapt.

these are stories.
I have never seen you run or leap.
you were old before I was born.

a few weeks after the service
a second widow stops to ask a question:
pastor, she asks,
when you bury my husband
would you leap across his grave too?

you did not laugh, though maybe you wanted to:
you did not tell her that leaping is not
part of the liturgy for the dead.

ii.

when I was twelve we came upon your car
in the ditch –

the baby blue sedan
flipped
like a beetle on its back,
tires spinning
you crawling out the window
with a finger of blood on your forehead
and a face flushed and pale as marbled beef.

you lived,
though you prophesied death
every sunday.
first from the pulpit,
then standing on the porch,
waving us into the gloam.

this is the last you'll see of me alive –

a mantra as familiar as
the pallet bloom of prairie fire
in late summer
and the tiger lilies you told us not to pick
because they only grow once.

week after week I sat in the back seat
and your son, my father, honked the horn
in farewell,
backed out onto the highway
where logging trucks
kicked up dust and gravel
until fifteen years later
the road was paved
and you were in the hospital.

I think you were afraid.

oma's eighty-sixth nativity.

you are supine,
surrounded by family,
the panoply of hospitals,
the machinery of grief.

she is absent.
she recalls little now.

not how you slept in separate bedrooms
or your voice like smooth liquor
and afternoon *kafe*, hearty as *nusskuchen*.
how you spoke often but mumbled and muttered
more than you spoke –

iv.

with your grandchildren you are gentle,
not always with your children.

schlaf schön, träum gut und gott beschützt dich.

you make the sign of the cross on my forehead.
your touch is light, like a child's.

v.

on sunday they take you off life support, leaving only
the leap, the cadence of your speechless breath.

ROCK PICKING

in fields surrounded by alder, willow
you picked rocks for a farmer one summer.
in the fallow you found an arrowhead
so sharp it sliced the tip off your finger:
blood fertilized the soil. you kept the stone
secret for years, sometimes you pulled it out,
held it in your hands, held it under
the light. you decided to show a friend –
but the arrowhead slipped from eager hands,
broke into casual pieces upon
the concrete floor. you didn't understand
metaphors for breaking, being broken.
you slept the whole afternoon through, ordered
a pizza, watched old movies until dark.

ROAD RACE, CHRISTMAS DAY

For Alex Decoteau, Chris and Junior

i.

a photo, 1910.
Edmonton before
the war.

some version
of the same cold
streets.

same regiment.

Alex Decoteau's eyes are closed.

one leg raised in anticipation
of next steps.

his hair is short
and black,

legs are bare.
the number three is on his
chest. faces line

the road.

ii.

the night before you left
it snowed.

some christmas lights hadn't
been put away
       yet.

christmas trees prone
       in back-alleys,

wrapping paper
       in see-through blue bags,

needles
       falling into snow.

iii.

before Decoteau's war
        the regiment found
a coyote in Saskatchewan.

they named him
        Lestock.

he mewled all the way
        across the Atlantic,

all the way to war.

the ship's captain said:
keep that damn dog quiet.

iv.

after skating Chris and Junior
asked when
they would see you again.

I don't know, you said. when I get back.

iv.

on christmas day Alex Decoteau floats
over snow

until seven years later
some german farmboy pulls the   trigger

and stops all
        anticipation.

his legs are
churned into mud.

spirit floats

over nameless bodies like
yellow smoke from elm-leaf
fires.

v.

you return to wet grass
and thunder.

Chris and Junior? the man from church says. haven't seen them in months.
            wait.
I thought one of them was caught up in some kind of drugs.

vi.

the city encroaches on
farm land.

coyotes encroach upon
the city.

CHURCH GOING

walk past the lintel
of your childhood

      church.

little has changed:

white, wood-panelled walls flung
up out of earth

under prairie sun
where flies crawl
on stained ceiling tiles
in summer,

winters so cold
that radiators
crack.

the people sing
a *mighty fortress is our god*
as sons and daughters walk

          down the stairs
       to sunday school

drift down the highway
in time.

the foundation too is cracked,
the basement smells of mould.

cheap prints of a victorian Jesus
testify on worn wooden walls.

he stands:
>   *bright-eyed with lantern, knocking at the door*

he kneels:
>   *man of sorrows weeping blood in Gethsemane.*

the carpet was replaced
ten years ago
by church council
after a potluck of beef chili
and ham sandwiches.

on weekdays the pastor takes lunch
at the chinese restaurant.

everyone knows his name –
that his order will include fries
           and a good tip.

he is old
           now too.

you've come to see the field
where your opa's body was buried –

but after announcements
and a hymn

you shake the pastor's warm, small hand
and pause outside

to watch dandelion heads
crushed fragrant on pavement,

flowers tossed by children at play.

POEM FOR THE DEAD AFTER WAR

a car accident takes
        the first,
cancer takes
        the second,
a suicide
        comes third.

these are simplifications.
the kind that are not
useful to anyone.

the dead are not
useful:

                they are
                dead.

you occasionally
see them on the
street –
heads bobbing in
sidewalk rhythm,
buying smokes,
stooping into cabs.
smiling.

they are dead:

you
do not think of them
often
most of the time.

POEM FOR THE LAST TIME YOU WORE
YOUR UNIFORM

his body
weighed
more
in the
remembering
than you
thought a
body could.

it was probably
the accumulated
mass of ten years
pushing down
on you –

a divorce, a few
doctor's visits,
a degree or two.

the boys you never
saw
again.

when he
was buried
you didn't
want to be
wearing your
uniform.

you didn't
want to be
wearing
anything,

but you shaved
one last
time, scraped
the skin around
your throat,
bled a bit
and drove
the hot highway
to Peers.

it didn't feel right.
things were
too green,
too overgrown,

rank with
weeds and heat.

dogshit in the
tall, dry grass.

the cameras were
out. the news
crews, the soldiers
and parents and
cousins.

everyone threw
lumps of
dirt into
the hole.

a cricket
jumped in.

the dirt
crumpled in
your hand.

dry, infertile.

you wanted
winter again,

a white
sheet over

everything.

you didn't
even get
drunk when
the funeral
was over and

ten years later
your dad
found the uniform
in a black garbage
bag at the back
of a closet.
forty dollars
in the pocket.
two twenties –
the old paper kind.

four dollars for
each year
that had passed.

OTTO AFTER THE WAR

Fritz, Otto, Peter and Paul eat canned sauerkraut in
Canada, a million sausages from home.

Fritz once brushed up against the *führer* but did not
engage in conversation for fear of the leeks he had

eaten for lunch. Otto was born in Berlin, raised in the
township of Michipicoten, never saw the war himself,

but his name alone was the fulcrum of a hundred
schoolyard fights. the beefy canadian boys laughed

at his accent and lunch, then *naziboy! naziboy!* grew
pale and sweaty like a glass of gewurztraminer, swung

his fists like christmas hams. the last time you saw Peter
he was foaming at the mouth, yelling at a homeless

man who said the pancakes Peter served in the shelter tasted
like microwaved shit (they did). and Paul, pronounced

Pow-ell, sings *lieder* in *lederhosen* at the german culture club,
trinkt too much, doesn't think about the war anymore at all.

SOMEWHERE IN FLANDERS/AFGHANISTAN

in Flanders Fields some shit
       went down –

flowers, crosses, the dead, etc. etc.
but the dead do not speak John.

sometimes they leave letters;
sometimes they leave a room full
of porn and candy wrappers
that someone else has to clean.

carthago delenda est, so on so forth.
you served our country, whatever
that means.

but I'm tired of hearing you go on
about birds and sunsets and torches
and god knows what else.

I'd rather meet your hundred-year-old
ghost on remembrance day.
when everyone's drinking to forget

the shit we volunteered to do
in a country that wasn't our own.

I'll buy you a beer though I don't really
drink much since my wife left,

don't sleep much either.

nobody sleeps well after
    war.

STIGMATA

cut two holes in a pillowcase
        and place it over your head.
look through the eyes of sixteen
        years, basic training. stand next
to the black soldier once more –
        head covered, arms around
his waist. watch the other soldiers
        laugh, force yourself to laugh
along. this photo exists in a reality
        you no longer understand.
the stigmata of race with
        and without hate. catalogue
the discomfort, place it in
        the cargo box next to your
bloody combat pants and
        the prone man on the road,
body holes blooming bright.

FOR THE SOLDIER WHO SLEPT
ACROSS THE HALL

Outside my windows, seagulls and crows continue
the discourse on language, insisting it need not be beautiful
to be song

– Kayla Czaga

i.

they tossed the blanket aside and snapped a photo:
        we laughed.
voices like casting lots, pixelated cotton,
strung-up digital

flesh.

he said he would tell the sergeant-major
if they didn't delete the photo. we laughed
        again.

ii.

the face of a small bird,
two tours in Afghanistan,
someone who hurt him as a boy.

you will never know why his mouth
curled to the right

or where he slept
when he showed up late
for work.

      he slept across the hall.

iii.

what you know

he drank too much one night –
hung himself from the cloth of his uniform.
more photos, an army investigation.
more strung-up, digital
      flesh.

iv.

he is buried.
you do not know where.

one day you will visit and the sun will be shining
and the snow will be falling and
you will stand and eat an apple
and remember how he shared his food

      with you.

ON TEACHING TIM O'BRIEN
TO AN AMATEUR HOCKEY TEAM

they titter when you read *fuck*
and laugh out loud when the lieutenant
talks about stroking Martha's knee
all night long. most wish to be
elsewhere: eating burgers, meeting
women, practising the motions that
will earn them bread and wine and
glory but today they are young
and sure of foot. after a loss
their faces wax tight like skin
over nectarine flesh but soften
with a win, and when Ted Lavender
is shot in the head outside Than Khe
they fall silent –
only to chortle again when you read
zapped while zipping, they giggle
and repeat; or *potted while taking
a piss,* they gloss, shuffling
laptops into bags; not seeing
that they are the boys in the platoon.
that they bleed with Ted Lavender
on the jungle floor, with Kiowa
on the ice at every small town arena,
on sand and asphalt overseas,
that boys in platoons eventually
die. the following class they are still
young and lost a game again.
you woke in the morning envying
the epistemologies of small

town arenas, the silver cold of winter
wheat, the way silence follows
those who are no longer alive. so you
cancel class, walk with them to the gym
and shoot hoops in sliding, socked feet.
the players are laughing at everything:
you are laughing the platoon to sleep

VISITING THE OLD FARM, ALBERTA

dry pines needles in sunlight,   morels in the shade

within a short time of arrival   your brand-new   iphone
                    slips   from shorts and   into the pond
with a flash
          of blue   like trout
                    released into the stream.

the barbed wire   strung so intentionally   across spruce
well   before   you were born,
          now enmeshed by still   growing   trees,
folded and fused   into belligerent saplines.

 cleaning out the garage
you find the owner's manual   for the 1967 snowmobile

          which is no longer *mobile*

               you chortle to yourself as you climb atop remember

          the smell and safety
of your father in winter. try to identify the various lichens
on metallic surfaces which will never move

          again.

a heron circles   wide   loops
 and the beavers build   a dam
                    the tawny specimen   that tows

a fresh poplar past your canoe   does not notice you
                or the noise of semis from highways nearby.

at dusk you sit in the empty house   with a window view

                of the dark and consider leaving
the city again.

  you wake hours later to the crack   of pileated woodpecker
        against an old telephone poll.
 when the light is gone you wander down to the pond
       and startle at electrical flashes when you thought you were

        alone –

       the fireflies you have not seen since a child
a loon call echoes across water   time.

STORIES YOU TELL WHEN YOU WISH
TO LOVE AGAIN

i.

two years together – she has a stroke.
he bathes and changes and feeds her.
she cannot speak thanks with stiff lips
or offer gratitude beyond who and what
she is. he cleaned the house before
the stroke but now he does it alone.
for ten years the two are twined,
till she passes beyond time or care.
he did not want thanks, he says:
he wanted her. he dies on a construction
site. their trailer is now empty. stinging
nettle grow tall in the summer sun,
teeming around ruts and wheel wells.
the neighbour's cows roam the warm
pasture, the air smells of chamomile.

ii.

the white-haired woman reaches out,
touches your beard at a fish and chips
shop out east – *Larry used to have a beard.*
she speaks without pause or inflection,
her eyes ocean blue. *they shaved it for the tubes.*
you look down at your plate, fingers thick
with grease. the door bangs shut, jangles
on the in-swing. from outside she waves
until you smile. the Atlantic rattles window
glass. she walks away, strong on her own
as the ocean, casting glances at the deep.

iii.

the soft whistle of an evening train,
freight car tattoos on rusted red grain
sheaves, Alberta blue, bright yellow lettering.
the heater kicks on clattering and softening
into a barely perceptible hum. his eyes contain
solitudes, the expanse of the land he was born
into. eighties synth pop blares from his speakers,
the album he was listening to when his brother
died. he misses his parents, the taste of seal.
standing at the head of his bed and closing
his eyes. he falls back on the mattress: *the feeling
of falling brings me back to my family*, he says and
offers you a beer, lights a cigarette.

VIEW FROM A SLIDE
YOU ONCE SLEPT UNDER

before time and war and other old gods
you slept under stars like a flapping owl
on the cooling crust of earth. your bones were
soft, your body without form. words of life
fell to the ground like burning globes of fruit,
you ate your fill; there was enough for all.
you flew with the wind, made love to the sun
whenever it asked, but the truth is this:
when you returned from the war, you didn't
think of the dead much. you wanted to be
a child again. you walked wide streets at night
alone, and counted stars under a slide.
owls watched you walk away at dawn, only
the owls were crows, their feathers wet with rain.

SUNDAY MORNINGS

it was evening all afternoon

— Wallace Stevens

when the mornings are all fresh ground coffee
fried egg sandwiches, sunshine on drapes
and Wallace Stevens oranges, you wonder how
Paul Nash would have painted Afghanistan –
soviet tanks in oil perhaps and the desert at night
with chalk or ink? Marilynne Robinson told you
that butter is the best foundation for an egg sandwich,
better than mayonnaise, and when the yolk
in the pan splits yellow, separates from butter and
solidifying whites, you start to think: the man in Kakfa's
metamorphosis must have been a soldier with his legs
blown off. how else could he hate himself so much?
not an easy question as you fill the cup again,
but you have both your legs. your concern resolves
into an Elizabeth Thompson sunrise over Kandahar
Airfield and the ice cream bars they had at the base
that you liked so much. ice cream aside, Kafka knew
something about soldiers, and before the war you saw
one fall from the table with food in his foaming mouth.
he writhed himself to calm on the concrete floor,
and it was all very startling, very much a Prince
Myshkin moment. he ended up not going to war.
the epileptic fits made his hands shake. you felt bad
but one clearly can't hold a rifle with shaking hands.
back then you still wanted to hold a rifle yourself,
though it never felt quite right, the metal was too hot,

your skin was too cool, but go to Afghanistan you did.
now you are back. you do not have blood on your pants
this morning. even the meat in the fridge is bloodless,
the bacon spits and hisses but the life went away long ago,
rubbed its grease on the corners of your couch, left a wet
snout print on the window. now you sit in the sun eating
a fried egg sandwich, writing sunday poems in the
complacencies of plaid pajamas, a white shirt: your face
is clean. you warm the coffee in Septimus Warren Smith's
cup and ask him how Virginia Woolf wrote things that were
so bloody true but he doesn't respond at all. so you turn on
netflix and it was *evening all afternoon* – or something like that.
you fell asleep and the house smelled of bacon fat and coffee
when you awoke.

REMEMBER YOUR BODY AGAIN

remember your body
  again –

how cedar smells of god
and a Bach cantata
makes you almost
forgive
your hands.

how your dad drove a
cream mercury cougar
while smoking cigars
and listening to
Leonard Cohen's
nineties resurrection

a room in an old
house with white curtains
where your mother drank
kafe in summer.

remember sweetgrass and
smoked moosehide

the embryotic hum
of a potter's wheel,
lego on the floor,
clay that stuck
to your mother's hair,
to your beard

to the creases
of your
hands.

remember your body
     again.

QUIET

as you try to sleep
take
twenty-nine years
       divide them
by metre sticks

arrive
       at the rain keeping you
awake.

A POEM IS NOT GUANTÁNAMO BAY

For Omar Khadr

a poem is not the man who crushed mint leaves
into milk and offered you lentils while you watched.
with rifle in hand.

it's not the door you kicked open or the woman
whose face was uncovered, the fruit on her table,
the flap of skin, the white-throated, fluttering chicken.

it's not the night you drove home drunk, though you
didn't then consider it as such.
it's not the diesel fuel and burning shit, the *get some!*
scrawled on plywood.

a poem is not a dream that refuses to stop, the man with
a hole in his foot, the Panjwai highway, the shards of corolla,
the man with a hole in his foot. a poem is not guilt.

a poem is not a way out of a poem.

a poem isn't even a decade later when you are not a soldier
and he is not in jail, when Guantánamo Bay is mostly
forgotten, when you meet for food at a local cafe.
it's not the musk of yerba maté, the bowl of rice and
chickpeas you share.

a poem is not a way out of a poem, but the bowl before you is
a bowl, and the chickpeas cooked only minutes ago. the table
   is next
to a window.
city trucks swath gravel off the street. a dog barks. it's slowly
growing dark outside.

EXODUS

I did not always hate.

I rub a ball of beeswax
between my hands
to remember
that hope is not
byproduct or waste,
but deep synteresis,
new words springing
from raw soil
after rain.

ACKNOWLEDGMENTS

Previous versions of some poems appear in *THIS*, *The Sugar House Review* (US), *The Literary Review of Canada*, *Word Riot* (US), *Prairie Schooner* (US), *The Nottingham Review* (UK), *Freefall*, *Alberta Views*, *Contemporary Verse 2*, *QWERTY*, *Ruminate* (US), *War Literature & the Arts* (US), *Matrix*, *The London Review of Fiction* (UK), *The Glass Buffalo*, *The Quilliad*, and *The Slow Wars* chapbook by Rubicon Press. Thank you to each of the editors. "Food habits of coyotes, as determined by examination of stomach contents" won the 2015 Glass Buffalo Poetry Contest. The title of the poem is taken from "Food Habits of Feral Carnivores: A Review of Stomach Content Analysis," originally published in the *Journal of the American Animal Hospital Association*. "Fruit on a wooden table" was performed as a spoken word collaboration with Maxine Courtoreille-Paul and Céline Chuang at the SkirtsaFire HerArts Festival. Permissions for excerpts have been provided by John K. Samson and Kayla Czaga.

I never thought of writing a book, much less a book of poems. *Slow War* came about because of the care of many people. Thanks to Lisa, Céline, Kurt, and Doug for early edits, Tim, Ruth, and Neil for teaching me to how to read books again, my family for always loving me, Johnny for a listening ear and a winged sewing machine tattoo, my local superstore for providing endless cans of club soda, my old Volvo for driving me around, my excellent editors at McGill-Queen's, and all of the friends, mentors, professors, editors, soldiers, and protesters who've walked alongside me during the difficult times and the good. I'll do my best to remember the soldiers who've passed away and the people of Afghanistan, for whom war is still a reality. My love to you all.